בס"ד

From CHILD to MAN

A Jewish Boy's Guide

S. Peysin

Published by
Targum Publishers
Shlomo ben Yosef 131a/1
Jerusalem 9380581
editor@targumpublishers.com

For questions, comments or suggestions,
please email guideforbochurim@gmail.com.

CONTENTS

Terminology 4

Introduction 5

The Changes that are Happening. 7

Opposites Attract 14

Care for Your Body 19

Every Body is Different 24

Emotional Changes 25

Personal Safety 26

Maturity. 29

Neshamah Maturity. 32

Resources: 34

TERMINOLOGY

You will notice that many words in this book are written in English, even though Hebrew words for these terms exist and are used throughout Torah and *seforim*.

Rashi often uses the term *"la'az"* when translating a word into Old French, which was the common language at the time. Such a translation aided in the understanding of the *Chumash*. *"La'az"* stands for *"lashon am zara,"* "the language of a foreign nation."

Being that English is an accepted and commonly understood language, we will use English words in this book in order to better explain these concepts.

INTRODUCTION

The time of your *Bar Mitzvah* is very important. It is when you are considered ready, *beruchnius*, to keep the entire Torah and *mitzvos*.

Before the time of a *Bar Mitzvah*, a boy is still considered a *Na'ar*, a youth. He is not responsible for any *mitzvos*, except in a way of *Chinuch*, educational learning. For example, even though you are not *mechuyav* in *kiddush* until you are *Bar Mitzvah*, you have probably said it many times. This is because you were learning and practicing for the "big game." If keeping Torah and *mitzvos* during the years before a *Bar Mitzvah* is considered playing the little leagues, a *Bar Mitzvah bochur* is like an All Star player!

Together with the readiness *beruchnius* for all of the important jobs of a boy who is *Bar Mitzvah*, like being part of a *minyan* and putting on *tefillin*, come the changes that start happening *begashmius* which change a boy's body from that of a child to an adult. The *mitzvah* of getting married, for example, requires an adult body.

You may already know about many of these changes, or you may be learning about them for the first time. These changes are called puberty and they can begin to happen any time between the ages of 10 to 15. This is also referred to as the time of adolescence. Puberty may take a few years and sometimes longer. One *bochur* might grow a full beard in the time that it takes for another *bochur* to just begin sprouting mustache hairs!

The time of puberty can be challenging, so being prepared can help you. It is important to understand and take care of your body, as well as to have people who can support you when you need them. Being close and open with your parents, having good friends and a *rav* who you can speak to are good tools for you to use as you go through these changes.

You may be excited, nervous, confused or uncomfortable with all the changes that are happening. It can be helpful to remember that everyone goes through it (even your parents and friends!), and it is a challenging time for everyone. Everything that you are experiencing is normal and just another part of growing up.

Wishing you much *hatzlacha*!

The Changes that are Happening

Here are some of the physical changes that will happen during puberty:

HAIR GROWTH

Hair will grow in the armpits, and on the area around the *milah*, known as pubic hair. This may start as light colored hairs, and will later grow thicker and darker. Hair may also begin growing on the chest, back and legs. Soon, the mustache and beard will start to grow.

This is an appropriate time to discuss the *minhagim* of your family and community regarding beard growth with your parents or *rav*. Remember that there are a number of *poskim* and different opinions on the matter. It may be helpful to learn the subject matter in the text.

PHYSICAL GROWTH

HEIGHT

You will grow taller during your teenage years, up to four or more inches in one year! This quick growth that happens in a short amount of time is called a growth spurt. When you finish your growth spurt, you will be your adult height.

Some boys have one big growth spurt. Others may have several smaller growth spurts during the years of puberty.

WEIGHT

You will gain weight, usually thirty pounds or more, during puberty. Your bones, muscles, and organs are all growing during this time.

If you are worried about your weight, talk to a doctor before going on a diet.

SHAPE

Your shoulders will widen. Your chest may become broader. You will become stronger, more coordinated, and more muscular during puberty.

If your breasts grow a little full or tender, this is normal. They will be flatter and not tender anymore by the time puberty is over. This condition is called gynecomastia and usually lasts for six to eighteen months. Up to half of all boys will get it, and usually around age thirteen.

Your feet and hands will grow longer and wider. This usually happens early in puberty. Your feet and hands may grow faster or finish growing before you see other puberty changes.

With so much activity going on in your body, it is common that some body parts may grow faster than others. Your arms and legs may grow longer and faster, causing your chest and waist to look too short. One side of your face may grow a little faster than the other. Your ears may look too large for your head. All these changes may cause you to feel clumsy and think that you look funny. Hang in there! This is all part of normal growth during puberty. Your body parts should match in size and length by the time your puberty has ended.

VOICE CHANGES

During puberty, your voice becomes deeper. The testosterone hormone causes this to happen. Testosterone causes your larynx or voice box to grow and your vocal cords to become longer and thicker. When your vocal cords are finished growing, your voice will stop cracking and squeaking. You will have a lower, deeper adult voice. The larger larynx may protrude from the throat, causing a lump sometimes called an Adam's apple.

(This term is actually based on a misinterpretation of a known story from the Torah, the story of the *Eitz Hadaas*. Many people believe that the *Eitz Hadaas* was an apple tree. Imagine that Adam got a piece of apple stuck in his throat, and you can understand how the protrusion of the larynx got its name!)

PUBIC CHANGES

The scrotum (pouch of skin containing the testicles, *Beyim*), and the *Beyim* themselves will grow. It will grow larger, coarser, and darker. The *Beyim* will hang loosely down. Usually this occurs first, followed by growth of the *Milah*, which will become longer and thicker.

The proper word for testicles is *Beitzim* (ביצים), which means eggs — so called because of their shape. However, to use a *lashon nekiah*, a more refined language, we refer to them as *Beyim*.

Similarly, there are lots of *kinuim* that refer to the male body part, the penis. In the Torah, we find the word *Zachrus* (זכרות), from *Rashi* in *Parshas Balak* 25:8.

Some families adopt their own term which they use when teaching young boys about their body and using the bathroom. Some use the word *milah*, *Bris Kadosh*, etc. In this book, the word *milah* is used.

This is one of the most important changes which will happen, and has the potential for the most *kedusha*.

When a baby is born, males or females are generally identical except for one organ — one body part; the *milah*. In English, the *milah* is known as the penis.

The very first *mitzvah* that you did was with your *milah*, having a *Bris Milah*. The tip of the *milah* used to be covered by a thick piece of skin, the *orlah*, known as the foreskin.

At a *bris*, the thick skin is removed to reveal a softer more sensitive area of the *milah*. In a way, this refers to revealing the more refined part of the *neshamah*, making us more receptive and open to Hashem, Torah and *Yiddishkeit*.

The *milah* is actually a very holy body part. In fact, according to the *Zohar*, before *Adam Harishon* did the *Cheit Eitz Hadaas*, a special light shone from the area of his *milah*. He was not ashamed of it. *Cheit Eitz Hadaas* caused him to feel uncomfortable with the private parts of his body, and he covered it.

The *milah* is the body part that is used as part of the process of having children. During puberty, the *milah* is preparing for its important job. You may think that you're a little young to be preparing for having children, but the *chiyuv* for marriage actually begins at *Bar Mitzvah*, along with the other *mitzvos*! Nowadays we don't actually get married at this age, because we are busy studying Torah and preparing for marriage.

So far in life, you probably knew of only one thing

See *Zohar Aleph* in the *Hashmatos 16b, gimmel 306b*. "Adam's heel (referring to his *milah*) dulled the orb of the sun."

that comes from your *milah*, urine, also referred to as *Ketanim* — the waste fluids that your body gets rid of when you use the bathroom.

However the *milah* is also the place that the *Zera*, semen, comes from. The word *Zera* literally means "seeds." Imagine that creating a new baby was like planting something. A new plant needs lots of things to grow, like good soil, water and sunlight. The *Zera* of a male is like the seed that is planted for a new baby to grow.

The word *Zera* is also used to mean "offspring" or the children that a person has, because that is what the *Zera* accomplishes. For example, we give people a *brachah* to have *"Zar'a Chaya V'kayama,"* "living and enduring children."

Zera is actually a combination of "sperm," which are microscopic cells, and fluid. The *zera* appears to be a whitish, yellowish fluid that is somewhat thick and it comes out in the amount of about a teaspoon or more.

Zera is produced in the *Beyim*, testicles, which are enclosed in the scrotum which hangs beneath the *milah*.

The task of the *zera* is very valuable (it creates new *Yiddishe* children!), and this is one important reason why we are very careful not to waste any of it. When *Zera* is wasted, even by accident, it is called *Zera Levatalah*, "wasted seeds."

Imagine if you were carrying a little handful of very rare and important seeds that were going to be used to plant a special fruit tree in the royal palace gardens. You certainly would be very careful not to spill or waste any of them! This topic will be discussed at length later.

More frequently during puberty, the *milah* becomes

Zera — זרע

hard. This happens when blood rushes to that area, and causes what is called an erection, known as *Kishui* (hardness, from the word *kasheh*). Because of the hormones of puberty, this may happen by itself, but a *bochur* must take care not to cause it to happen deliberately.

We will discuss some details and practical tips on this later.

HOW DOES PUBERTY HAPPEN?

Physically, during puberty, some important hormones are working in order for all of the changes to happen. A hormone is a chemical that flows around the body through the blood and causes a change or effect in the body.

One of the most important male hormones is testosterone. The brain sends a message to the *beyim*, which begin to produce testosterone. When the amount of testosterone in the body starts to rise, it causes the body to grow and change, as well as produce *zera*.

Your doctor can be a good resource to answer any of your questions about puberty and your changing body. If puberty begins to happen at too early an age, around nine years old, or does not seem to begin by age fourteen, a doctor could determine if everything is normal.

If you have any pain or swelling in parts of your body, or something just doesn't feel right, don't hesitate to ask a doctor about it. After all, that's their job!

Kishui — קישוי

OPPOSITES ATTRACT

There is a well known expression that "opposites attract," like the opposite forces of a magnet. This expression applies very much during the time of puberty when boys begin to feel an attraction for girls. This is normal, and it should not be considered bad to *have* these feelings, although it is not the time to express them. Because a man needs a woman in order to get married and fulfill the *mitzvah* of "*Pru Ur'vu*" by having children, Hashem created an attraction between males and females.

There are lots of explanations for why this feeling exists. The easiest one to understand is right from *Chumash Bereishis*. When Hashem created Adam *Harishon* he was the only person by himself. When he felt lonely and wanted a partner, Hashem made Chava from a part of him. There is even a *Medrash* that Adam and Chava were created back to back and only later separated. Because Hashem took away something from Adam and used it to make Chava, Adam felt that he needed to be close to Chava in order to feel complete again. This is the way every man feels when he comes closer to the time of

---

Pru Ur'vu — פרו ורבו

being ready to get married.

To avoid improper behavior before marriage, there are many *halachos* and *hashkafos* regarding these feelings of attraction. At the time of marriage, it will be appropriate to express these feelings, but before that time, a person should be careful to guard himself by looking, thinking and speaking only about proper things.

SHMIRAS EINAYIM
(GUARDING THE EYES)

Has it ever happened that you saw a picture that made you feel happy, sad or scared? The things what we see are very powerful and can cause us to have feelings.

Shmiras einayim means being careful to look at only appropriate and *tznius'dike* images; whether on signs, in magazines, videos or real life. The things that you see remain in your memory forever, so be sure to fill your brain with only proper images! There is also an idea of *Shmiras Einayim* when you go to the *mikvah*.

In the *Gemara* it says that the *pasuk* "*Velo Sasuru Acharei Eineichem*" also refers to not getting distracted by inappropriate thoughts. If that happens, a person should right away try to think about Torah, or even better, to learn some Torah inside or to *daven* from a *siddur*.

SHMIRAS HALASHON
(GUARDING THE TONGUE)

No, this is not just about *Lashon Hara*! The *Chachomim* tell us that we should guard our tongue from speaking about these sensitive subjects when it is unnecessary. Even just speaking about them can be interesting, but it can lead to improper thoughts or behavior.

This also means that if someone feels it is important

to discuss these issues, they should carefully choose who to speak with.

SHMIRAS NEGIAH
(GUARDING THE TOUCH)

The *Chachomim* made it *asur* for boys and girls to touch each other over a certain age. For girls, the age is three, for boys it is nine or even earlier. Some *poskim* allow *negiah* under certain circumstances, such as to shake hands for business, and others do not allow it at all.

There is also a concept of *yichud*, that girls and boys of the ages mentioned above are not allowed to be alone together, whether it is in a closed room, or even outside in a private place. *Yichud* is permitted between mothers and sons, fathers and daughters, as well as other family members.

The *halachos* of *yichud* can be complex, and there are many *seforim* which address practical scenarios in which you might find yourself!

SHMIRAS HABRIS
(GUARDING THE BRIS)

The concept of *Shmiras Habris*, keeping your *bris* (or *milah*) holy includes the *issur* of *Zera Levatalah*, wasting *zera*. We mentioned before that *zera* is special and we take measures to try and not waste it.

It is *asur* to waste *zera* by masturbating, which means stimulating or touching the *milah* to cause *zera* to come out. The *taavah* (desire) for this can be extremely strong, which is a sign that your body is preparing well for adulthood and marriage!

Kishui always occurs before *zera* is released, but if someone has *kishui* for any reason, they can distract themselves and the *kishui* may go away on its own.

What you think, see, hear or talk about may also make it hard to control the *taavah* for *Zera Levatala*.

Being that it can take some time to understand how your body works, most people make mistakes until they figure it out. That is why it is also called *Chatas Ne'urim*, the *aveiros* of youth, since it is so common for youth to slip up in this area at least once.

Sometimes *Zera* will come out without you doing anything. When this happens at night while you are sleeping, it is called a *Mikreh Lailah*, "something that happens at night." In English, it is known as a "nocturnal emission" or a wet dream. This is a normal occurrence and happens to all young teenage boys, some more than others.

If this happens, you can simply change your clothes and sheets and go back to sleep. You may feel more comfortable to do your own laundry for this reason.

Although a *Mikreh Lailah* technically happens by itself, and the person may not have actually caused it, there are things that can help prevent it.

Often, things that are thought about during the day are dreamed about at night, which may cause a *Mikreh Lailah*. Having numerous instances of *Mikreh Lailah* could indicate that a lot of time is spent thinking certain thoughts.

Following the advice of the *Shulchan Aruch* of which position to sleep in can also help prevent a *Mikreh Lailah* from happening.

Being tempted to do things which lead to *Zera*

Mikreh Lailah — מקרה לילה

Levatala is part of puberty and the growth process of becoming an adult.

It is very normal to be interested in such things, and these feelings are part of every person's body, in the same way that you get hungry or sleepy! The Torah says "*Bocheh Lemishpechosav,*" that the Yidden cried when Moshe commanded them about these things, because they knew how hard it is to control yourself! It may be the most difficult thing to do in your life.

There are a number of sources that speak about the *issur* of *Hotzaas Zera Levatalah,* such as the *Shulchan Aruch, Rambam,* and *Gemara.* You may want to look these up yourself, or learn them with your father or rav.

Here are some practical ways to keep yourself on track:

- Try going to sleep only when you are very tired, and sleep in a room with someone else or at least with the door open.
- Do lots of activities! Exercise, hobbies, sports, spending time with friends, doing schoolwork and getting involved in *chesed* projects all help keep your mind on more appropriate things. Of course, keeping your mind on Torah, which should be your most important goal during these years, is a great protection for yourself.
- Staying in a *tznius* environment, and avoiding certain books and videos is very helpful. If you know of things that cause you to have thoughts and feelings that may lead to *Zera Levatalah,* those are the things that you should stay away from!
- Choose your friends. Spend time with people that encourage personal *kedusha* and influence you in a

positive way.

- Adding in *Yiddishkeit* by *davening* better, and even checking your *mezuzos* and *tefillin* can protect you. There is also an idea of saying the first four *perakim* of *tehillim* before going to sleep.

Each time that you are successful in maintaining your personal *tahara* should encourage you. It is not possible to promise yourself that you will never make a mistake; trying to be ALWAYS perfect can make you too nervous to succeed each individual time! Take it just one step at a time. If you make a mistake, you don't have to start all over again or feel bad; just try again.

It is well-known that when Hashem wanted to give the Torah to Yidden, the *malochim* claimed that they should receive it because they are so holy and could appreciate it more. However, Moshe Rabbeinu argued successfully that they wouldn't actually be able to keep the *mitzvos*! If the *malochim* had the Torah, they would never had made mistakes. Instead, Hashem gave the Torah and *mitzvos* to us, and we are not perfect like *malochim*! Because it is a struggle for us to keep the *mitzvos*, each time we do the right thing we give Hashem much joy and should feel a sense of personal accomplishment!

The struggle that each person has with *Shmiras Habris* is individual and private. It is something you may want to discuss with a trusted rav, older sibling or parent.

CARE FOR YOUR BODY

Exercise and healthy eating are important as your body grows and changes. Your growing body may require more food and healthier varieties.

Cardio exercises, which increase your heart rate, such as walking, jogging or swimming are important activities to keep your growing body in shape.

Also, be sure to sleep well every night. Getting enough sleep allows the mind to focus and develop properly, as well as giving the body the strength it needs to function.

CLEANLINESS

Wash your body regularly and as often as necessary. Use soap or body wash, and shampoo. For more oily hair, you may need to shampoo often. For dry, flaky scalp, called dandruff, you may want to use specialized dandruff shampoo. After showering, be sure to put on clean clothes, especially undergarments!

ATHLETE'S FOOT

Athlete's foot is a foot condition that is common in athletes but can happen to anyone who has wet or sweaty feet. It causes the skin to become itchy, cracked and painful, especially between the toes. Sweaty feet can have a bad odor and become a breeding ground for athlete's foot.

To prevent athlete's foot, it can help to wear socks with high cotton content and shoes made of natural materials. Be sure to change your socks daily, and allow your shoes to dry between wearings. Also, dry your feet well whenever they become wet. Using a powder that absorbs the moisture can be a good idea.

Athlete's foot is contagious. Don't walk barefoot in places where people with athlete's foot may have walked. Flip-flops are cheap, and can go a long way in helping prevent you from catching the disease.

Athlete's foot can be treated by a number of creams and sprays that are available over the counter.

JOCK ITCH

Just like athlete's foot, jock itch is a contagious fungal infection, and just like athlete's foot which doesn't only happen to athletes, jock itch doesn't only happen to jocks!

It happens for the same reasons though. When the groin area or upper thighs are confined in sweaty materials, not dried properly, and irritated from the friction of clothing, it can cause the red, itchy, dry rash known as jock itch.

Jock itch is treatable using anti-fungal creams and sprays, but the best thing to do is try and prevent it. After a sweaty ball game or on a hot humid day, be sure to wash and dry your body well. Don't share towels and clothing with others, and if you have athlete's foot, make sure that clothing and towels don't touch from one area to the other. Change your clothing, especially undergarments, daily.

DENTAL CARE

Usually by the age of twelve, all of a person's baby teeth have already fallen out and the new ones grown in. We are starting with a new, clean slate of brand new teeth. If you had many cavities in your baby teeth, you can now start afresh with your new set.

In childhood, the main concern of caring for teeth is in brushing them well. Children are educated in brushing teeth with toothpaste, preferably twice a day or more. In adolescence, the concern shifts to gum care, and preventing periodontal problems, especially as the hormones which cause puberty can also affect the gums. (*perio* — around, *dontal* — teeth.) This is accomplished by flossing at least once a day, before brushing the teeth. The more often, the better! Flossing cleans out food particles that get stuck between the teeth, often causing cavities in those hard-to-reach places.

Teeth are attached to your gums by tiny fibers. Once those fibers are destroyed by germs, they cannot be replaced and the tooth will become loose. It is therefore extremely important to care for your teeth on a consistent basis. Gum disease happens because food that is stuck between the teeth hardens after thirty-six hours and the germs affect the fibers holding the tooth. After this time, the food debris cannot be removed. It must be removed when soft, by flossing.

Note that the floss does not need to be "sawed" between the teeth, rather, care should be taken that the floss passes between each of the teeth.

Also, every six months, it is a good idea to visit a dentist for a dental checkup and cleaning. A dentist can address any problems when they are small. It may be interesting to know that a dentist can instantly tell if a person flosses regularly or not! So if you want to impress your dentist or hygienist, you will need to floss more often than just the day of your appointment!

Brushing your teeth is also important socially as it makes your teeth appear clean and your breath smell good. This is especially important if you are learning *b'chavrusa*!

It is also recommended to use a mouthwash to clean bacteria from your mouth and to have fresher breath.

ACNE

Acne, known as pimples, will usually start early in puberty. The skin of your face is actually made up of many tiny follicles, almost like little holes. Each hole has a gland which produces an oil called sebum. The hormones of puberty can cause the glands to produce too much oil. Pimples happen when oil from the face and little pieces of dead skin and bacteria get stuck in a follicle causing it to redden and swell. Pimples can be cared for by washing your face at least once daily, sometimes more often, especially if you are exercising or sweating. You may notice that certain foods or kinds of soap make your acne worse.

If you have further concerns about your acne or skin condition, a skin doctor called a dermatologist may be able to help you, using certain face rinses, creams, or medications.

BODY ODOR

During puberty, the apocrine sweat glands which are in hairy areas of the body become active. This is why adults sweat more than children, especially in the armpit and pubic areas. Bacteria will usually be present in sweaty areas, causing body odor. It will be necessary to shower more frequently, as well as use deodorant. Wearing deodorant is important to prevent and neutralize body odor. Even if you may not be aware of your odor, the people around you most certainly are, especially when you are learning and *davening* in a crowded room or *shul*!

There are a number of deodorant options, including sprays, roll-on, and stick options, with various scents and strengths. If you aren't sure, enlist someone's help in choosing the right one for you.

PROTECTING THE *BEYIM*

The *beyim* are a very sensitive part of your body and should be protected from damage. During certain sports and activities it is a good idea to wear a jockstrap and "cup" which cover and protect that area.

These can be purchased in most department stores, and in any sports equipment store.

Every Body is Different

With everyone around you going through puberty at the same time it is common to start comparing your changing bodies. Being the tallest, strongest, fastest or having more facial hair may suddenly seem important.

When you look in the mirror or spend time with friends, keep in mind that there is no "perfect" appearance or ideal body. Whether you are stronger or weaker, taller or shorter, smarter or not as smart does not determine your success or self-worth. Every person is a special, unique individual, and perfect in their own way. Don't spend time comparing yourself to others or wishing that you could be different. Hashem creates each person exactly the way that they are meant to be.

When it comes to yeshiva or sports there will always be those who are faster and those who are slower, but everyone should feel comfortable to participate and have fun no matter what their skill or level. Be sensitive of those around you, and make sure that everyone is included in games and learning without emphasizing differences.

Emotional Changes

In addition to all of the physical changes you are experiencing, you may also notice some emotional changes. You will start having more adult emotions, which can be more intense and take time to get used to.

Adolescence in general is a time of change in many ways. It is common to feel more upset, frustrated, confused or angrier than usual. It is also common to have mood swings — quickly changing from one mood or feeling to another.

This can be just as hard on you as on the people around you! It can affect your relationship to your parents, friends and Hashem. Use these opportunities to understand yourself better and find ways to improve your mood.

Being more sad than usual is called depression and to some extent it is a common condition. Feeling a little "blue" is normal. Eating well and getting regular exercise, fresh air and sun can help with that. But if someone feels so depressed that they can hardly get out of bed in the morning or function properly, it is important to see a therapist who can suggest certain thought exercises or lifestyle changes which can help. In some cases, medication may be prescribed.

Personal Safety

The word molest means to bother someone, especially in a hurtful way. Molestation refers to when someone behaves inappropriately with another person without their permission or consent.

Often this has to do with touching or showing the private parts of the body, but any touch you don't want can also be molestation. For males, it may involve the *milah* and backside.

Anyone who breaches your boundaries is doing a very wrong and hurtful thing. A molester could be anyone, even a rabbi, teacher, doctor or someone you consider a friend or a friend of your family. It could happen anywhere; at home, school, camp and *shul*.

A person who was molested *Chas Veshalom* might feel embarrassed, upset, scared or even guilty, as if they did something wrong. It could affect them physically, emotionally, mentally and spiritually, even many years later. However, nothing you do can justify molestation.

Unfortunately, this could happen to anyone, which is why we need to be aware of it so that we can be careful. It is important to know that no one is allowed to touch you or even speak to you in a way that makes you feel uncomfortable, even someone that you know very well and trust.

If you feel uncomfortable with something, even if you are not sure what it is or why, you should tell the person to stop, and try to get away from them.

Many times, a molester may threaten someone that they are going to do something bad to the person or to their family if they tell what happened. This is just a trick that they might use to keep it a secret and it shouldn't prevent you from telling on them.

A molester may also say that what he is doing is a special secret. Even if you aren't sure what happened or why, you should feel safe to tell someone you trust.

Other types of improper behavior may include inappropriate exposure or showing of a person's private parts. As mentioned above, anything that makes you uncomfortable or just doesn't feel right should be stopped right away, and a trusted adult should be told about it.

There are many people who are available to help someone who was molested. If a person was molested, they should be sure to tell their parents, *rebbi* or principal or anyone else that they trust right away. They should not be worried about telling on the person who did it or be worried that others may not believe them.

It is important to tell someone as soon as possible, so that the molestation will not happen any more and to make sure that the person who did it will not be able to hurt anyone else.

Many *poskim* have ruled that it is not *lashon hara* to tell on a molester and that it is *halachically* the right thing to do.

SOVRI Helpline is a *frum* service that takes

anonymous calls to help anyone who was molested: (888) 613-1613

QUICK TIPS:

- You are in charge of your body, and what is private stays private.
- No one is allowed to talk to you, joke with you, or touch you in an inappropriate way.
- If you are uncomfortable with someone's touch, behavior, or manner of speech, you are allowed to ask them to stop and expect them to do so.
- If, *Chas Veshalom,* someone tries to molest you, tell them to stop and go tell a trusted person.
- If, *Chas Veshalom,* molestation occurred, it is not your fault. You can feel safe to tell on the molester.

Maturity

It's a good thing that growing up is a process. Imagine if people went from being newborn babies to instantly being adults! People need time to adjust to changing shape and changing abilities. It can't just happen overnight, and the truth is that growing and maturing never really stops.

People can always learn more, act nicer and discover new things. When you are younger, learning and changing happens very quickly. In fact, the fastest year of development is the very first year of a baby's life. Their body grows very quickly and they learn all kinds of skills like smiling, laughing, rolling over and crawling in a very short time. There are also changes that you can't see happening, but are very important. Babies learn to recognize people, remember favorite toys and food, and experience many different kinds of feelings.

This is a lot like the changes that happen during puberty, both inside and out. You can see the physical changes that your body is going through, and you may also realize that the way you think and feel is changing too. Being able to control your impulses, asking thoughtful questions, and caring more about other people are signs of maturity.

People will expect you to act more maturely, and in some situations or with certain people it will be easier than others. How people behave in different situations tells a lot about them. When visiting friends or family, take the opportunity to practice helpful and proper behavior.

Be sure to greet people in a friendly manner and offer to be helpful. When eating a meal at someone's house make yourself available to help with table setting and serving or entertaining the kids. "What can I do to help?" is a great question that shows how eager you are to be helpful. Demonstrating good table manners makes a mature impression on others.

When it comes to conversation, less is more! Being a better listener is more important than having lots of things to say. If you are asked to speak or tell a story, use the opportunity to improve your speaking confidence within a reasonable amount of time.

With your advancing age comes lots of fun and new responsibilities. You probably get to stay up later, participate in grown-up events, and will be trusted more at home and at school. You may want to spend more time with your friends and away from your family. Balancing your new freedom will take a lot of maturity and thought. When the *Yidden* were freed from *Mitzrayim*, they were no longer the slaves of Pharaoh, but became servants to Hashem, responsible to keep the entire Torah and *mitzvos*. Is that called freedom? It sure is. Freedom doesn't mean free-for-all. A person who does whatever he or she wants is really a slave to themselves. The best kind of servant to be is a servant to Hashem, which means following the Torah.

When you are experiencing freedom, keep in mind the consequences of your actions. Especially when your parents aren't around you will need to be extra careful to make good and safe decisions. By following the laws of the Torah, the laws of the country, and keeping to your own personal standards of safety and maturity no matter what other people are doing, you will enjoy your freedom in a happy, healthy and responsible way.

Neshamah Maturity

When you were young, your parents tried to instill in you a love of Hashem, Torah and *Yiddishkeit*, as well as *yiras shamayim*. They washed *negel vasser* with you, said *Shema* and *brachos* with you, helped you kiss the Torah in *shul* and enjoy *Shabbos* and *Yom Tov*.

Once you reach the age of *Bar Mitzvah*, you start doing these things on your own. It is no longer the responsibility of your parents to make sure you do so, as you are considered an adult according to Torah.

During the time of adolescence, as the brain develops and you become more independent, it is common to question things that you have learned or done in the past and wonder about the future.

Part of this is because your intellectual capacity actually does increase! That's why the *Mishna* says that the age of *Gemara* learning is fifteen, when a boy is capable of the abstract kind of thinking needed to properly understand *Gemara*.

Once you are able to think on a deeper level, the simpler explanations that you were given as a younger child might not seem like enough anymore. You may want to seek out explanations that satisfy you on your current level.

For this reason, a *Bar Mitzvah* boy is entrusted with the responsibilities of the Torah. This will be the time in life that you choose a path of Torah for yourself, in a personal way.

May Hashem give you success in all the areas of your life, so that you can live and enjoy a life of Torah and *mitzvos* in the best way possible!

RESOURCES:

נדה: י״ג א

נדה: מ״ו א

בבא קמא: פ״ב א

יומא: י״ח ב

משנה תורה, הלכות איסורי ביאה, כ״א:ט, י״ח

רמב״ם (ווילנא) על משנה סנהדרין, ז:ד:א

שלחן ערוך אבן העזר, כ״ג:א

שלחן ערוך אורח חיים, ג׳:י״ד